B. P. Pratten

Chile and Spain

The whole question officially stated: part 1, the question settled, part 2,

the question reopened

B. P. Pratten

Chile and Spain
The whole question officially stated: part 1, the question settled, part 2, the question reopened

ISBN/EAN: 9783337245016

Printed in Europe, USA, Canada, Australia, Japan

Cover: Foto ©ninafisch / pixelio.de

More available books at **www.hansebooks.com**

CHILE AND SPAIN.

THE WHOLE QUESTION

OFFICIALLY STATED.

———◆———

PART 1.—THE QUESTION SETTLED.

PART 2.—THE QUESTION REOPENED.

———◆———

NEW YORK:
1865.

SYNOPSIS OF DOCUMENTS.

PART 1.

The Question Settled.

No. 1.—Spain's formal complaint against Chile, as presented by the Spanish Representative, Mr. Tavira, on the 13th May, 1865.

2.—Reply of the Chilian Government, May 16th, 1865.

3.—Acknowledgment of the receipt of this reply by Mr. Tavira, and statement that the explanations contained therein are satisfactory and " dissipate, in his judgment, all the motives for complaint which his Government had entertained."

4.—Acknowledgment of the receipt of this reply by the Chilian Minister.

PART 2.

The Question Reopened.

No. 1.—First note of Admiral Pareja, in which he reopens the whole question, disavows the previous action of the Spanish Minister, adds to the previous demands of Spain, and peremptorily requires full satisfaction within four days, under threat of the immediate rupture of diplomatic relations and a resort to force.

2.—Copy of the powers under which Admiral Pareja acts.

3.—Reply of the Chilian Minister of Foreign Affairs, in which he repeats the full explanations before given to Mr. Tavira, but protests against the character of Admiral Pareja's demand, and repels his threat to resort to force.

4.—Admiral Pareja's final dispatch to the Chilian Government, in which he announces that he shall resort to force if his demands are not complied with within 48 hours.

5.—Final protest of the Chilian Government.

PART I.

THE QUESTION SETTLED.

No. 1.

The Claims of Spain as First Presented by the Spanish Minister.

LEGATION OF SPAIN IN CHILE, 13th May, 1865.

YOUR EXCELLENCY : The unpleasant events which occurred in this place about the first of May of the past year, by reason of the Hispano-Peruvian question, obliged me, as the Minister Resident of Her Majesty near your Government, to transmit to you the notes dated 4th, 13th, 23d and 28th May, 8th June, 4th July, 21st and 27th September, 6th and 26th October, 12th, 23d and 24th November, 7th and 15th December.

Your Excellency addressed to me in reply those dated 14th, 15th, 28th and 31st of May, 4th and 7th of July, 24th and 29th of September, 4th and 24th of October, 7th, 8th, 19th, 28th and and 29th November, and 14th of December, of all of which I gave opportune information to Her Majesty's Government.

The pacific and friendly solution of the Hispano-Peruvian question has occurred to justify what I always told Your Excellency, that it was an isolated fact. If your Government did not accord to this the assent due to it, if the press erected imaginary phantasms to have the pleasure of combatting them, and misled public opinion, and Your Excellency did not think proper to impose on it the wholesome correction which you might within the bounds of law, I will not for that fail to congratulate myself for having fulfilled my duty. The word *correction* I have used generally in the notes of which I have made mention, and I have arrived at the persuasion that you did not give to it the true and genuine meaning, because were it not so, I should not know how to account for it that Your Excellency could not interfere with the extravagancies of the press and of public opinion, without infringing any law, having at your disposal the official newspaper, the parliamentary tribunal, &c.

On the very day I noticed with pain that moderation and propriety were far from being the guides of all the publications.

I, who as the representative of Her Majesty, in the early days of the contest limited myself solely to uttering pacific assurances, and proper protests in defence of the rights of my nation, will not pass beyond the limits of moderation and justice on account of the constant intemperance of some writers, most of all when results have justified my forecast and loyalty. The deplorable events pointed out occasioned special action, in compliance with what is settled in article 12 of the treaty concluded between Spain and Chile, which says ; " The Republic and her Catholic Majesty desiring to maintain the peace and good accord which happily has now been re-established by this present treaty, declare solemnly and formally ; that if, (which God forbid), the good understanding which ought to rule in the future between the contracting parties should be interrupted through want of comprehension of the articles here agreed upon, or for any other cause of offence or complaint, neither of the parties shall be authorized to sanction acts of reprisals or hostility by sea or land without having presented beforehand to the other a justificatory memorial of the motives on which it founded the injury or wrong and the denegation of competent satisfaction."

I place before Your Excellency that the Government of Her Majesty believes, that the Government of the Republic has infringed the law of nations, the treaty aforesaid, and that it has given offence.

1st. In that measures were not taken to avoid affronts given to its flag on the 1st of May of the year last past, as your predecessor, Mr. Manuel Antonio Torcornal, offered to me, and the commandant of the municipal battalion, who remained impassible in front of the legation, making his troops mark time during the act, was not brought to trial.

2d. In that your predecessor made to the Hispano-American Republics the protest of the 4th of May of the previous year, thus infringing what is settled in article 12 of the treaty between Spain and Chile.

3d. In the Government not applying the wholesome correction to observations of public opinion within the limits authorized by law, and urged upon it by duty.

4th. In that in proportion as it allowed the Peruvian war steamer "Lerzundi" not only to take in supplies of coal, provisions and powder, but also to establish a bounty on the enlistment of seamen, (of which it took off three hundred men, a few more or less, who were allowed to embark after the port was closed), it placed obstacles in the way of sending off supplies to Her Majesty's squadron.

5th. In that it did not order the institution of the preparatory proceedings asked for by me to investigate the truth as to the expedition of volunteers who assembled at Valparaiso, armed and uniformed, and announced by all the newspapers, it permitted to go from that port for the coasts of Peru in the "Dart;" and in that the Intendant of Valparaiso and the Chief of Police refused to detain the arms, clothing, munitions and medicines of the expedition on the verbal application of the Vice-Consul of Her Majesty at that port.

6th. In that it did not take the measures necessary to remove the fear diffused among the peaceful inhabitants of the republic by the anathema fulminated through the defamatory libel called *San Martin*, in the third number of the 7th September, in which it menaced with the popular anger every one who should supply the Spanish vessels or their agents with even a single pound of flour, a lump of coal, a drop of water, &c.

7th. In that the "Vencedora" having arrived at Lota, (doubtless because of the foregoing anathemas), was treated as an enemy, coal, &c., was refused to her, and the maritime Governor disregarded the protest of her commander, and, in the Government having issued the decree of the 30th September, approving the conduct of that functionary, instead of instituting proper preparatory proceedings for investigating such an unusual transgression, in order to proceed according to law.

8th. In that the Government declared coal to be contraband of war, with the object of prejudicing Spain and belligerents against this country and Peru, knowing it was not, and without considering that it put itself in contradiction to what the Minister Plenipotentiary from Peru said on the 4th of July last.

9th. That the Government of the country knew that Spain was not in declared war with Peru, while it was evident that the French empire was with the Republic of Mexico; that Spain, by the 10th article of her treaty with Chili has the right to be treated as the most favored nation, by which it ought at least to enjoy for the supply of its squadron the same franchises as are conceded to the Empire, and therefore, it is, that as the slightest obstacle was never opposed to the Empire supplying itself with coal, munitions and provisions directly, (such was prohibited to Spain,) the treaty was infringed.

10th. In that, after the Government had declared itself to be neutral between Spain and Peru, it permitted for account of the latter the purchase of horses, and their embarkation on three occasions at Valparaiso, notwithstanding they are declared contraband of war by the law of nations.

11th. In that, notwithstanding my conclusive notes of 21st and 27th September, 6th October, and 7th and 15th December, the Government did not take the measures which the law authorized it to do against the defamatory libel called *San Martin*, the most indecent which to this time has issued from the most degraded press.

The Government of Her Majesty, which holds as the rule of its conduct that every one jealous of his own honor should look to that of his allies as his own, will be willing to receive the solemn declarations which the case demands, provided they are compatible with its dignity.

I reiterate to your Excellency the assurances of the distinguished consideration, with which I am

Your obedient and faithful servant,

SALVADOR DE TAVIRA.

To the Minister of Foreign Affairs of Chile.

No. 2.

Reply of the Chilian Government.

DEPARTMENT OF FOREIGN AFFAIRS FOR CHILE,
SANTIAGO, 16th May, 1865.

Sir:—I have had the honor to receive the note which, under date 13th of this month, you have been pleased to address to me, in order to place before me that the Government of Her Catholic Majesty believes that the Government of the Republic in the course it has pursued since the 1st May, of the year last past, by reason of the Hispano-Peruvian question, has done a wrong to it, at the same time that international law and the treaty existing between the two countries are infringed. At the same time you signify to me that the Government of Her Catholic Majesty, which holds as the rule of its conduct that every Government which is jealous of its honor should regard that of its allies as its own, will be disposed to receive the solemn declarations which the case demands, provided they are compatible with its dignity.

In the note referred to, my Government sees, with regret, that its frank and well meant policy during the by-gone Hispano-Peruvian conflict has been appreciated in a manner little favorable to it, but is justly gratified in observing the enlightened spirit of conciliation which moves that of Her Catholic Majesty to desire, as mine does, a solution, friendly and satisfactory to Chile and Spain, of the difficulties which at present paralyze their good understanding, although in the correspondence which it fell to me to have the honor of maintaining with you through the course of the year last past, are to be found expressed at large the causes to which the pending difficulties owe their origin, as well as the legitimate motives which determined the action of my Government in the complications between Spain and Peru; my Government makes it a duty to enter into a fresh examination of the facts to which you call its attention. I venture to hope that this fresh examination, inspired by the honor and dignity of the Republic, will achieve the rectification of the opinion of your Government in regard to the sentiments

2

of mine, and will place in clear light that, far from purposing to fall short of the duties which, in regard to Spain, the law of nations and the treaty of recognition and friendship which it has concluded with it, impose on it, the Government of Chile has deplored as you do, the unpleasant events which have occurred, and most especially the publication of the *San Martin*, and has known how to fulfill completely those duties, under all circumstances and despite the thousand impediments it has found in its way.

But it is necessary that the Government of Her Catholic Majesty should persuade itself that the anomalous mode employed for the occupation of the Chincha Islands by the agents of Spain, and the strange principles proclaimed to that effect, were the cause of all that has occurred. In those proceedings, in the impressions which they produced on the country, and in the conjectures to which they gave place, you should seek the explanations of all the incidents. My Government would also turn to make an investigation and analysis in detail of such irritating causes, if it were not for the desire to keep at a distance occasions for recrimination of every nature, and if it were not its belief that every motive for complaint should disappear before the explanations which I pass on to give to Your Excellency with the frankness and loyalty never swerved from by the Government of Chile.

To the incident which happened on the 1st of May, of the year last past, in front of the residence of your Legation, my Government cannot suppose that you would attribute importance to it, except for the note addressed some days afterwards by you to this Department. In view of that it hastened to collect the information requisite to an estimate of the nature and gravity of the case, and from this it appeared that the incident was owing to an inconsiderable outburst of the moment, by good fortune suppressed in the very act, and to an entirely accidental circumstance. The battalion of the National Guard which was present on that occasion, far from authorizing, or by its presence encouraging any offence to the Flag of Her Catholic Majesty, was the first to prevent or repress it. In fact, on the day cited, an assembly of the people was together in the municipal theatre, part of the crowd which was going to it paused inadvertently in front of the house occupied by Your Excellency, and in doing so some odious cries were heard. But these cries, called forth by the excitement produced by the recent accounts of the events at Chincha, and inevitable in every numerous assemblage, in which excitable temperaments are never lacking, found no echo from the majority of the meeting, nor were they followed by any act derogatory to the flag of your Legation. If any intended it to infer such, they were restrained from their punishable purpose by the assemblage itself, which thus gave unequivocal evidence of its discretion and good conduct. The assemblage made no delay in pursuing its course, pressed forward by the battalion of National Guards present at the time, which by marking time behind it, evidently intended to avoid any misbehavior which could have been intended against the flag of Spain, and to hinder the assemblage by remaining there a length of time, from becoming changed into a tumultuous mob. From what is here stated it follows there was no reason for bringing to trial the Chief of the battalion referred to, whose conduct at that meeting was, on the contrary, worthy of eulogium; and that the flag of Her Majesty received no insult. If such had been received, my Government would have been very severe in punishing the authors of so great disrespect, having regard as well, not only to the dignity and privileges of a friendly nation, but also to the dignity of the Republic. Happily it confides too much in the intelligence and good sense of the country it governs, to fear that it can ever forget the inviolable respect due from every civilized people to the flag of friendly nations.

For the rest, sir, you are not ignorant of the measures which were taken some days after this popular effervescence, that such scenes should not be repeated, and you could hoist your flag with the same security that you now do.

My Government cannot discover in what the circular it addressed to the other Governments of America under date of 4th of May last past, can be contrary to the stipulation of Article 12, of the treaty in force between Chile and Spain, neither could the treaty have deprived my Government of the right to estimate acts which, like the occurrences at Chincha, had such immediate relations with the tranquillity, independence and welfare of the Republic, nor was it within the condition of the article alluded to. At that moment my Government confined itself to examining and demonstrating the anomalous conduct of the agents of Her Catholic Majesty, and to manifesting its confidence that the Cabinet of Madrid would not place the seal of approval on such conduct. Inspired by a legitimate forecast, and by a sincere desire to maintain the good understanding between Chile and Spain, that circular met with the adhesion and sympathy of all the Governments of America which have with Her Catholic Majesty alliances more or less close, and was in part corroborated by the declarations of the Cabinet of Madrid itself.

Your Excellency knows very well that in Chile the periodical press is placed beyond the reach of all official influence, and enjoys very ample liberty for the utterance of its opinions. No less ample is the liberty which all citizens have to meet and discuss every matter having an interest more or less general. Public opinion, through the multiplicity of its means of expression, through the substantial guaranties which the political constitution and other laws of the Republic hold out to it, and through the difficulty of condensing estimates and convictions into homogeneous order, would have evaded any efficacious corrective, even in case my Government should have coincided in judgment with Your Excellency, that it would have been salutary and proper to have imposed such.

My Government is gratified to observe that you now agree with it in opinion that the best *corrective* of the errors of the press, is to be found in the press itself, and thanks the explanation of your idea, perhaps not previously understood in its genuine and true meaning, for being able to rectify the construction which it attributed to you when you indicated the use of extraordinary measures to apply the due corrective to extravagancies of opinion.

When the Peruvian war steamer *Lerzundi* arrived at Valparaiso, Peru had not declared herself at open war, nor in actual hostility towards any nation, and if part of her territory was in the occupation of the Spanish squadron, she appeared to await the determination of the Cabinet of Madrid about such occupation, before taking measures to put an end to it by open force.

Notwithstanding this, data in possession of my Government
warrant it in affirming that the *Lerzundi* did not ship at Valparaiso articles of war, except only the men necessary to make
up her crew, and the provisions she had need of, to return to
her port of destination.

Nor is the conduct of my Government less justified in respect
to the expedition which left Valparaiso, bound for Callao, on
board the Chilian schooner *Dart*. That expedition consisted
of a certain number of volunteers, who left the country with the
purpose of passing over to Peru. In such a purpose there was
nothing illicit or punishable, since the form in which it was proposed to execute the purpose could not change the nature of its
character. If these volunteers could have passed over to Peru,
in exercise of a lawful right, in the line of steamers, what reason could there be that they might not do so in sailing vessels?

But it is added that they carried arms and munitions on board
the *Dart*, and entertained the project of attacking vessels of the
squadron which occupied the Chincha Islands. This circumstance might impress a different character on the expedition, and
although nothing could be more unlikely or incredible than such
a project, orders were nevertheless given to the authorities at
Valparaiso to prevent the departure of the *Dart* until it should
be ascertained that neither arms nor articles of war were carried
on board of her—orders which were duly and exactly complied
with.

As to hindering the departure of the volunteers themselves,
that could not have been done without infringing the laws of
the Republic, which permit all its inhabitants to leave the country at their pleasure, and without any restriction. With less
reason could they have been subjected to the action of the courts
on the mere rumors which the daily press put forth about the
objects of the voyage.

You think that my Government ought to have taken
measures necessary to remove the fear diffused among the
peaceful inhabitants of the Republic, by a certain anathema fulminated through the paper called *San Martin*,
against those who furnished supplies to the Spanish ships. The
adoption of such measures would have assumed that some importance was attributed to, and some influence conceded in, the

public opinion of the country to the publications in a newspaper whose character very soon brought it into contempt in the eyes of the public. Little, therefore, could it influence the mind of any, or engage the attention of my Government, by which the anathema in question was passed completely unnoticed.

To have regarded, as you would have wished, the protest of the commander of the *Vencedora*, the maritime sub-delegate at Lota would have had to compel by force the holders of coal to sell a quantity of the article. That would have been to violate the most valued guaranties which the laws of the Republic secure to private interests and persons. If the holders of coal, yielding to the apprehensions and alarms which were everywhere caused by the occupation of Chincha, or for reasons of another sort, refused to supply a part of their merchandise to the *Vencedora*, the maritime sub-delegate could not avoid that, by subjecting them to a forced sale. There is less reason to infer from this that this functionary was disposed to act with hostility towards the *Vencedora*, insomuch as this vessel, while she remained at Lota, could freely repair damages, supply herself with provisions, and take in ballast. You can very well understand that, had the sub-delegates of Marine been disposed to be hostile, the schooner would not have had facilities for any of these operations. As little can it be concealed from your penetration that it would have been very easy for the owners of the coal, by placing an exorbitant value on the article, to elude any order of sale which they might have received from the maritime sub-delegate, who in such case would find himself compelled to submit to seeing his orders mocked, or to have recourse to deciding himself the price or selling value of the article, causing to the owners a compulsory transfer of property unjustifiable and illegal, and violating in this respect the guaranties which the Constitution and the laws of the Republic grant to persons, to property and to industrial pursuits. The religious respect which all its governments have always maintained in Chile for property, is one of the sanctions which do most honor to the Republic, and should most commend it to the consideration of all civilized nations.

It was natural that the sub-delegate at Lota should give an account of his proceedings, and that in an affair of such gravity, foreign to his ordinary jurisdiction, and really unusual for him, he should desire to know the opinion of his Government.

The frank and explicit approval which it gave him, as it will always give when the conduct of its agents is adapted to the rules of the fundamental charter and the laws, cannot be a ground of complaint on the part of Spain, which in any like case, my Government is pleased to think, would have proceeded in an identical manner.

The diverse aspects which, in its course, the Hispano-Peruvian conflict presented, imposed successively on my Government a different attitude, and placed it in a peculiar situation.

Thus, whilst on the 4th of July, 1864, of the year last past, although it could not be considered that between Spain and Peru a state of war was actually existing, yet it was obliged to judge of things in a very different manner on the 27th September of the same year, when it issued a declaration about fossil coal. Then the Government of Her Catholic Majesty had already resolved to maintain the possession of Chincha, and for that purpose had sent to the Pacific considerable reinforcements, while on the other hand Peru showed a disposition to regain by force the islands occupied.

The indefinite and anomalous condition of former days had changed, through the acts mentioned and the explicit and grave opinions of the Peruvian Government, to a state of war or of actual hostility, which imposed on my Government the duty to make on its part a formal declaration. With the resolution determined on, my Government proposed to itself not only to meet loyally the duties of that neutrality in which the latest events had placed it, but also to place difficulties in the way of war, whose fatal consequences none of the belligerents would have been able to arrest. On issuing that declaration, therefore, it did not fall into that contradiction that you point out, nor in putting it into practice did it show itself to be partial to either of the belligerents.

If the ships of war of Her Catholic Majesty could not supply themselves with coal at the Chilian ports, as little was it lawful to supply it to the vessels of the Peruvian squadron.

For the rest, the right of my Government to make the declaration we are treating of, cannot be put in doubt. The law of nations does not settle anything binding as to what is the description and the character of stone coal. The divergence which exists on the subject reigns in the practice of the principal maritime powers, and in the doctrines of publicists, leaves every country in position to choose in the manner it may judge most in conformity with equity and the general principles of knowledge. But you observe that the ships of war of the French nation continue to enjoy in the Republic this franchise, even after the declaration of the 27th September, and notwithstanding that Empire is at open war with the Republic of Mexico. If the case had occurred it would have been completely distinct. For many years back France has maintained permanently a naval station in the Pacific, composed of a less or larger number of vessels, which are accustomed to take supplies, coal and other provisions in the ports of Chile. On the other hand, my Government has never even been notified, in an official or authentic manner, that any of the ports of Mexico on the Pacific were blockaded by the French squadron on account of the war waged there between the Republicans and Imperialists.

You find another cause of complaint against the Republic for having permitted the purchase of horses in Chile for account of Peru, which on three occasions were shipped at Valparaiso. In this respect I will remark, that Peru has always been accustomed to buy in Chile the horses she had need of, not only for the service of the army, but also for the labors of husbandry and industrial works. If in war on land this article can be considered as contraband, there is no reason for so esteeming it in a maritime war, which is the only one that can be made by Spain. On the other hand, the Peruvian Government could not export from Valparaiso a quantity of gunpowder, which it held in the care of a commercial house at that place, notwithstanding it was bought before the conflict in which, at a later day, it found itself involved. This case is sufficient to show the sincere loyalty with which my Government has fulfilled its obligations of neutrality.

Finally, you complain that the Government of the Republic had not taken the measures which the law authorized to punish the unworthy and base outrages which the periodical called *San Martin* directed against the person of Her Catholic Majesty. The measures which in this case my Government could take, were narrowed down to accusing the periodical in question be fore a jury through the competent judicial functionary, before your request. The resolution which should be adopted in this case was of a nature so delicate and serious, that although my Government might well suppose what might be your wish, it thought it prudent to be informed of that wish, in a decisive and express manner. For its part, it would have deemed itself forgetful of the consideration due to the sovereign of a friendly nation, by placing before a jury insults and affronts which needed not a condemnatory verdict to render them in the highest degree despicable and odious.

Avoiding such an irritating emergency, it considered that it should regard the honor and dignity of a friendly sovereign with the same solicitude as it would its own, which it has never deemed compromised by the severe attacks of which the members of the administration are repeatedly the object of the periodic press. It always has held, and holds the impression, that it was not incumbent on it to determine the attitude which, in the presence of events, it might best become the Government of Her Catholic Majesty to assume. In this it is supported by the confidence it feels of having given proof of consideration and friendship, in its testimonials of deference to your wishes in respect to this unpleasant incident.

In the re-examination I have made of the various incidents which have given matter for our past dissensions, I flatter myself that I have dissipated the causes of complaint set forth by you, and the doubts which might sustain Her Catholic Majesty's Government as to the real sentiments which animate the people and Government of Chile, in respect of Spain. The present explanations, which can only corroborate those which I have before given you, are a fresh testimonial of the constant yearning and efforts of my Government for the maintenance of the relations of friendship with Spain, and for the removal of every obstacle which might obstruct the re-establishment of a cordial understanding between the two countries.

Be pleased to accept the reiterated expression of the distinguished consideration with which I am

Your very obedient humble servant,
ALVARO COVARRUBIAS.

To the Minister Resident of Her Catholic Majesty.

3

No. 3.

Acknowledgment of the Spanish Minister that the Explanations of Chile were Satisfactory.

LEGATION OF SPAIN TO CHILE, }
SANTIAGO DE CHILE, 20th May, 1865. }

YOUR EXCELLENCY :

I have had the honor to receive your note dated 16th of the present month, in reply to mine of the 13th of same. I have seen therein with great satisfaction that the same wishes animate your Government as that of Her Catholic Majesty, to arrive at a solution, satisfactory and honorable to both countries, of the difficulties which have clouded their good understanding.

The sentiments which have actuated your Government amid the unpleasant events which have occurred, and the full explanations which you have pleased to give me on the eleven points on which Spain considered herself offended by Chile, dissipate, in my judgment, all the motives for complaint which my Government entertained, and will contribute, as I hope, to draw closer together the relations between the two countries.

I shall make it my duty thus to advise the Government of Her Majesty, in order that the sincere understanding which has always existed between Chile and Spain may not again suffer the least alteration.

This has been and will be the constant aim of all my action.

I renew to you, Sir, the distinguished consideration with which I am

Your obedient, faithful servant,

SALVADOR DE TAVIRA.

To THE MINISTER OF FOREIGN AFFAIRS OF CHILE.

No. 4.

Final Note of the Chilian Minister.

Department of Foreign Relations of Chile,
Santtago, 21st May, 1865.

Sir,—I have the honor to communicate to you the receipt of the note which, under date of yesterday, you were pleased to address to me, making known to me that the contents of my communication of the 16th instant dissipates in your judgment the motives for complaint which the Government of Her Catholic Majesty believed it had against the Republic, and will aid in drawing more closely together the relations between the two countries.

Such result will correspond with the wishes of my Government which has been gratified to learn your opinion on the communication alluded to. Please accept the testimony of the distinguished consideration with which I am

Your Excellency's obedient and faithful servant,

ALVARO COVARRUBIAS,

To the Minister Resident of Her Catholic Majesty.

PART II.

THE QUESTION REOPENED.

No. 1.

First note of Admiral Pareja. He re-opens the whole Question.

HEADQUARTERS *Flag-ship of the Pacific Squadron.*

The undersigned, Commander-in-Chief of the naval forces of Spain in the Pacific, and Minister Plenipotentiary of H. C. M., as shown by the annexed copy of full powers which have been conferred upon him. has the honor to inform II. Exc., the Minister of Foreign Affairs of the Republic of Chile, that he has been ordered by his Government to address to him the present communication, caused by insults offered to Spain, the satisfaction for which, as accepted by the Minister of H. C. M., Mr. Tavira, has neither met, nor could meet, the honorable demands of Spain.

Mr. Tavira having been recalled and his conduct severely censured, inasmuch as the note, addressed by him to the Government of this Republic on the 20th May last, openly conflicted with the instructions of the Spanish Government, in which note he accepted as a sufficient satisfaction the explanations contained in that of Mr. Covarrubias, dated 16th of the same month; it becomes the duty of the undersigned to reiterate the complaints already presented, relative to the conduct pursued by the Chilian Government, which has been systematically hostile to Spanish interests, since the origin of the conflict happily terminated between Spain and Peru.

Although your Excellency must be well aware of the nature of the events which have occasioned the present attitude of Spain towards Chile, still, nevertheless, it suits the purpose of the undersigned to recall the principal of these facts. The most prominent grievances are the following:

1st. That the insults and seditions words pronounced against Spain in front of the house occupied by the Spanish Legation did not receive their proper chastisement, remaining unpunished, not only the authors of the scandal, but also those who could have prevented it. Amongst these figures the commander of the civic battalion, on whom a heavy responsibility falls for having coolly witnessed the affray in the presence of his soldiers, and instead of impeding its continuance, if only by persuasion, limited himself to watching their proceedings as a disinterested spectator.

2d. The publication of the obscene periodic *San Martin*, whose columns daily overflowed with gross attacks against Spain and its dearest objects, was the cause of the repeated claims of Mr. Tavira, and although the laws of the Republic allowed only a small space for the Chilian Government to prevent the daily abuses committed by the above mentioned paper, it could, nevertheless, by explicitly condemning the opprobious articles brought to light with the sole determination of exciting unjust odium against Spain, have controlled the indicated publications. Not even in this indirect manner would the Government of Chile satisfy the demands of the Spanish representative, and on that omission the Government of H. C. M. found their complaint.

3d. The Peruvian war steamer *Lerzundi* met with every facility for providing herself with everything necessary in the ports of Chile, as well as articles expressly declared contraband of war. She was allowed to post her placards of enlistment, and recruited three hundred individuals.

The Government of Chile denies that the enlistment was extended over and above what was absolutely necessary for the navigation of the vessel; but in opposition to this negative, destitute of all proof, appears the unusual publication of the announcement of enlistment, when this is solely made use of for recruiting for men-of-war.

4th. The determination of the Government of Chile to declare coal contraband of war, affected in a most prejudicial and injurious manner the interests of Spain; and in view thereof, as also from the fact that the said declaration was unfounded, the Representative of H. C. M. seasonably protested against it, although his just representations were unheeded.

In defence of the act of which I now speak, the Government stated, that, taking into consideration the difficulties existing between Spain and Peru, and these being equivalent to a declared war, it was one of the necessities urged upon her as a duty; but the fallacy of this argument shows itself on observing that under precisely the same circumstances to which the Chilian Government alludes, the Peruvian war steamer *Lerzundi* provided herself with all necessaries, on the ground that no actual declaration of hostilities had taken place between Spain and Peru.

True it is that the Chilian Government pretends to make a distinction between both cases, under the supposition that on the 4th of July, last year, the war, subsequently declared on the 27th September, in virtue of the resolution of H. C. M. Government to continue the occupation of the Chincha islands, had not been declared. This, which constitutes the distinction above mentioned, is not so exact and truthful as it at first appears, nor does it meet the object indicated by the Chile Government; the continued occupation of the Chinchas is to be considered as a coercive measure, urging the prompt arrangement of the Hispano-Peruvian question and not as an act of conquest, as it has been proved by the manner of their evacuation.

The Chincha Islands were occupied by the Spanish forces when the affair of the *Lerzundi* took place, so that if the occupation of that part of the Peruvian territory is their only reason for qualifying this fact as the cause of the conflict between both nations, then it is necessary to acknowledge that if no war existed on the 4th of July, neither could it do so on the 27th September, as pretended by the Chilian Government.

The result of the foregoing argument is, that the law by which coal was declared contraband of war, was not founded on legitimate causes; consequently its effects having been detrimental to the interest of Spain, the Government of H. C. M. have every right to consider the said law, as a most unfounded and grevious offence.

Although the declaration to which I have just alluded deprived the Spanish squadron of the means of obtaining the coals necessary, still at the same time vessels of the French Navy, committing hostilities against the ports of another State of America, continued in the full enjoyment of free use of the ports of Chile, the same being denied to the naval forces of Spain.

This notable difference occurring between two nations, both finding themselves in an analogous position towards that Republic, constitutes another grievance; the gravity of which is not to be destroyed by the pretended want of official notification to the Government of Chile, of the blockade of some of the Mexican ports of the Pacific—since, granting the said want to have occurred, its publicity alone should have been sufficient to authorize the same deportment to both Spanish and French men-of-war.

It appears unnecessary to the undersigned to continue making mention of the various other complaints entertained by Spain against Chile, as he considers them sufficiently well justified in the documents of Mr. Tavira, and merely limits himself to reproduce them in this communication in obedience of the orders received from H. C. M's. Government.

Having clearly defined the causes that have originated the present attitude assumed by the Spanish Government towards Chile, it is my duty to manifest to your Excellency that the aforesaid offences have aggravated by the lapse of time that has intervened, Spain not having received any of the satisfactions claimed by her honor and her dignity; and that the conduct of Mr. Tavira, in not having carried out, in word and deed, the instructions received, by accepting the note of Mr. Covarrubias, as containing satisfactory explanations, not having been approved; the Government of H. C. M. considers that affairs are in the same state as when Mr. Tavira addressed to Mr. Covarrubias his note of 13th May last.

In virtue whereof, the undersigned has been ordered by his Government to demand of the Republic of Chili, that in due satisfaction of the complaints set forth by the representative of II. C. M., and recapitulated in this communication, satisfactory explanations be given on each of the points to which they refer, and furthermore that the Spanish Flag be saluted with 21 guns by one of the sea-coast ports, which salute will be answered with an equal number of guns by one of the ships of this squadron.

If the Government of the Republic should not accede to this just request, it solely will be responsible for the consequences, inasmuch as the Government of II. C. M. is firmly resolved to obtain the satisfaction it so justly demands in reparation for the insults offered to it.

Finally, the undersigned must represent to your Excellency that, if at the end of four days, counting from this day, no answer is received thereto, he will consider all diplomatic relations at an end between Spain and Chili, and all persons attached to the Legation of II. C. M. will repair on board of the flagship of he undersigned.

And should it become necessary to make use of the force under his command, which he would deeply regret, he will consider it his duty to demand an indemnity for the expenses sustained by the Spanish squadron by reason of the steps taken by the Government of Chili; an indemnity which, although the Government of II. C. M., yielding to a feeling of moderation peculiar to its character, does not see fit to claim, except in the extreme case of having to resort to force, it does not therefore relinquish its due right, which it is the duty of the undersigned here most solemnly to record.

The undersigned would deem it his duty to claim indemnity for all injuries which the subjects of II. C. M. resident in Chile may suffer in their persons and property, but whilst so doing he cannot but express the hope that whatever emergencies may arise the Government of Chile will check all attempts of a kind unbefitting civilized nations.

4

The undersigned embraces this opportunity to offer your Excellency the assurance of his distinguished consideration.

Given on board the Frigate *Villa de Madrid*, September 17th, 1865.

JOSE MANUEL PAREJA.

To H. E. the MINISTER OF FOREIGN AFFAIRS OF CHILE.

No. 2.

Powers under which Admiral Pareja acts.

FLAGSHIP OF THE PACIFIC SQUADRON.

Dona Isabel, by the Grace of God and the Constitution of the Spanish Monarchy, Queen of Spain, etc., etc.

Whereas, in order to terminate and settle the differences pending between Chile and Spain, in consequence of the grievances and insults offered to Spain in that Republic, owing to the non-compliance with obligations which civilized nations mutually owe each other, it may be necessary to enter into arrangements with the said Republic in order to determine the proper satisfaction; it being necessary that I should to that end duly authorize a person who, by his zeal for my service, may deserve my royal confidence, and you, Don Jose Manuel Pareja y Septiens, well deserving of the country, Knight of the Grand Cross of the Royal Order of Isabel the Catholic, Commander of the Royal and Distinguished Order of Charles III., twice Knight of the Cross of San Fernando of the First Class, decorated with that of the Navy of the Royal Diadem, Commander of that of Saint Gregory of the Pontifical States, decorated with the medal of Pius IX., Senator of the Kingdom, and Commander-in-Chief of the Pacific Squadron, etc., etc., uniting the qualifications necessary therefor, I have resolved to choose and appoint you, to the end that you may, in the character of Minister Plenipotentiary, concert and settle with the Plenipotentiary appointed by the President of Chile what may be most suitable and opportune. And whatever you shall thus concert, settle, treat, conclude, and sign, I ratify beforehand, and will observe and execute, and will cause it to be observed and executed, as if concerted, settled, treated, concluded, and signed by myself, for which purpose I give you my full power in the most ample form required by law. And in testimony thereof I have caused the present to be issued, signed with my hand, sealed with the privy seal, and countersigned by my first Secretary of State.

Given in the Palace of San Ildefonso, this twenty-fourth day of July, Anno Domini one thousand eight hundred and sixty-five.

I, the Queen, [seal].

MANUEL BERMUDEZ DE CASTRO.

A true copy.

JOSE MANUEL PAREJA,

No. 3.

Reply of the Chilian Minister of Foreign Affairs.

DEPARTMENT OF FOREIGN AFFAIRS OF CHILE.

Santiago, September 21, 1865.

The undersigned, Minister of Foreign Affairs, had the honor to receive on the 18th instant, at 6 P. M., from H. Excellency, the acting Charge d'Affairs, of H. C. M., the note dated 17th instant, addressed to him by Don Jose Manuel Pareja, in his double character, as Commander in-Chief of the naval forces of Spain in the Pacific, and as Plenipotentiary *ad hoc* of H. C. M., wherein he informs the Government of Chile, in obedience to the orders of his own Government, that the latter has deemed unsatisfactory the explanations contained in the note of the undersigned of the 16th May last, and accepted by H. Excellency the resident minister of H. C. M., in his note of 20th of the same month, for removing insults which Spain pretends to have received from this Republic. Mr. Pareja consequently recapitulates the charges already presented by Mr. Tavira, would explain away some of them, and finally asks of the Chilian Government satisfactory explanations on each of the points therein referred to, and also that one of the sea coast fortresses of this Republic shall salute the Spanish Flag with 21 guns, the Chilian Flag receiving in return a similar salute from one of the vessels of the squadron under his command. If this demand is not acceded to within four days, counting from the date of his aforesaid note, he will consider diplomatic relations between Chile and Spain as broken off, and if it should become necessary to make use of the force under his command, he will deem it his duty also to demand indemnity for the losses suffered by the Spanish squadron in consequence of the measures adopted by the Government of Chile.

The undersigned has laid the above communication before His Excellency, the President of the Republic, and in compliance with his instructions now proceeds to answer it.

It has been matter of remark and surprise for the Government of Chile that that of Spain should have entrusted the commander of its squadron in the Pacific with the management of the present affair, when it has in the Republic a legation through whose medium it could have discussed it in a more appropriate manner. The full powers, a copy of which has been forwarded by Senor Pareja to the undersigned, do not invest the Plenipotentiary with the diplomatic character that he would in strictness require in order to enter into official relations with the Government of Chile. If the Government of H. C. M. has hoped to render her demands more effective by entrusting the management of them to the Commander-in-Chief of her fleet, they have labored under a grievous error, and have fruitlessly deviated from the course usually pursued by enlightened nations bound together by solemn treaties.

Relying upon this informality, Chile might under other circumstances have declined giving the reply demanded by Senor Pareja, but, at the present moment, its failure in so doing, might be interpreted as a dilatory and evasive expedient, to which it is far from wishing to resort. On the contrary, it is her anxious desire to arrive as soon as possible at a clear and definite result, and she therefore has resolved to answer the present communication.

As regarding the substance of the documents received, the Government sincerely regrets that the Cabinet of Madrid should have deemed the aforesaid explanations insufficient and censure the course adopted by Mr. Tavira in accepting them ; but believes that this judgment, much at variance with its own, does in no manner affect it, nor does it authorize them to carry things back to the state in which they were, previous to the 13th of May last.

Not being aware of the tenor of the instructions received by H. C. M.'s resident Minister, and naturally supposing that his acts were in conformity with them, we placed implicit confidence in his official actions, believing them, as we did, to emanate from the representative of the public faith of Spain in Chile. Consequently, the arrangement of the difficulties existing between the two countries was looked upon as a thing of the past, since Mr. Tavira declared on the 20th May last, that the explanations given by the undersigned removed all obstacles, and also corroborated said declaration by hoisting again his national flag, which he had not done for several months.

Although Mr. Roberts, actual Charge d'Affairs of H. C. M. had received information to the effect that the conduct of his predecessor would not be approved of, nevertheless he hoisted the colors of Spain on Sunday, the 17th instant, a day of festivity ; and also on the following day in friendly homage to the 18th, as the glorious anniversary of our Independence. By these means he satisfied us that all difficulties were overcome. Nor could it be otherwise ; since, if Governments have a right to annul the contracts entered into by their ministers in foreign parts, all diplomatic relations would be without object, and without foundation ; and would become so uncertain and frivolous as to lay the world open to the artifices and abuses of any unscrupulous nation.

Although it were possible to pass over so grave a consideration, another of graver importance still presents itself. When on the 13th of May last, Mr. Tavira made known the motives of complaint Spain had against Chile, he limited himself, in order to remove them, to the simple request that the Republic would give a formal declaration compatible with the honor of the Government of II. C. M. to whose instructions, he stated, he was conforming himself in the demand.

The declarations were made by the undersigned, and accepted as satisfactory by Mr. Tavira; and even admitting that the Spanish Government could undo them now, they have no right whatever to increase their first demands, and all the more so when the grounds on which they were made have not been aggravated. To day, Mr. Pareja reproduces the motives of complaint then presented, and nevertheless, when Chile was only asked for declarations, now she is asked for satisfactory explanations, and a salute in reparation for the Spanish flag.

And in what manner are these new demands, which are not sustained by any new grounds of complaint, presented? They come through the medium of a peremptory, threatening and aggressive ultimatum, in which not even the forms of benevolence and civilization have been observed, presenting themselves on the very day of happiest memory for all Chilians, at the time of our great national festivity, as if it were wished to strike a new blow by hurting the patriotic sentiments and dignity of the nation.

Proceedings of this nature reveal a most marked hostility, and a desire to humiliate by every means in their power an almost disarmed country, without maritime forces, simply because she had confided her defence to her sense of rectitude, equity and moderation, and had consecrated all her efforts towards the benefitting and enriching of her country. The undersigned cannot conceive how the Government of II. C. M., through Mr. Pareja, renews claims which have been completely dissipated by his repeated and detailed explanations and the more when said claims are of themselves contradictory and incompatible. A claim is brought against the nation, for the facilities with which the *Lerzundi*, one of the steamers of the Peruvian navy, met for obtaining provisions in Valparaiso and completing her crew, assuming as a fact that Spain and Peru were in open hostilities. Yet, nevertheless, Mr. Pareja makes room for another claim, under the supposition that no such war existed, on account of the declaration of 27th September, 1865, respecting coal.

The truth is, that when the *Lerzundi* was in Valparaiso, there were motives for believing that peace existed between the two nations, as afterwards there were for believing the contrary on the publication of the afore-named declaration.

The affair of the *Lerzundi* took place before the Spanish Government had given Peru to understand its resolution to maintain the irregular occupation of the Chinchas, when the chief who consummated said act revealed that the step he had taken was not authorized by the Government of Madrid; in fact, in the meantime, the representative of Spain in Chile qualified the said occupation as an isolated act not approved of by his Government, and Peru, in the expectation of a different resolution, appeared not to desire to make use of force to retake the islands.

The declaration respecting coal took place, on the contrary, after the last Government, informed of Spain's unexpected resolution, seemed to be determined to bring to an end the Spanish occupation by force of arms, as is proved by the solemn records of the Peruvian Congress, the official declarations of the Minister of Foreign Affairs of the same Republic, and other public and unequivocal acts.

This is the true state of the facts, and in view of it the conduct of the Government of Chile is completely logical, justifiable, and faultless. To take any other view of it, is to invert, as Mr. Pareja has done, the order of events, and to suppose a state of war between Peru and Spain while peace existed, and peace when the other had come to prevail.

In order to found another charge on the decree touching coal, it is alleged that on the issuing that decree Spain and France were in the same relation to Chile, since, if the former was carrying on hostilities against Peru, the latter was doing the same against the ports of Mexico; and yet that the latter went on taking fuel in ports of Chile while it was refused to the Spanish armada. To give force to this charge, already considered and set aside by the undersigned, an evident error is committed; a state of civil war, the only war that prevails in Mexico, even though one of the parties be aided with foreign arms, is compared as identical with a state of war between two nations independent and sovereign, as Spain and Peru.

If the Government of Chile needed to add strength to the arguments employed to answer this charge, it would remind you that it rests on a fact at once uncertain and destitute of proof, to wit: That any vessel of the French squadron destined to blockade Mexican ports has taken coal or any other article contraband of war in Chilian ports. For its own part it is without information to this effect, and cannot accept a surmise as the basis of complaint.

There is no greater consistency in the charge brought against the Republic for the occurrence of May 1st, last year, at the door of the Spanish Legation. However much that occurrence may be regretted, it did not involve any outrage to the flag of Spain, as the undersigned has already had the honor to manifest in his correspondence with Mr. Tavira. So certain is this, that it has been impliedly recognized by Mr. Tavira, by the Government of H. C. M., and even by Mr. Pareja himself. Offences to the flag of a nation that respects itself are of such gravity as to make any relations between the offender and the offended utterly impossible until reparation has been fully made. If the Spanish flag had been outraged, and without reparation to this time, Mr. Tavira would not have continued in relations with the Government of Chile, nor even have continued residing in the country; neither would the sovereign of Spain have repeatedly directed in the course of the past year notice of events both prosperous and adverse which affected her royal household; nor would Mr. Pareja himself have styled Chile a *friendly nation* in the treaty which concluded the occupation of the Chinchas; nor would the Government of Spain have approved that expression, which no later event has occurred to change or make less appropriate; nor finally would Mr. Roberts, the present Charge d' Affairs of H. C. M., have unfurled his flag at the door of his residence, both on the last holiday and on the 18th of September, the glorious anniversary of the National Independence. While all these events have occurred, and are manifesting that no outrage can exist incompatible with the continuance of harmony and any sort of relations with Chile, they come notwithstanding to ask of the Government of the Republic a salute in apology to the Spanish flag.

Another charge as inconsistent as the preceding is that made against the Government of the undersigned for not having explicitly condemned in the official journal the tirades of the paper

San Martin. It were difficult to invent censure more explicit than what is contained in the notes of the undersigned touching that publication, and also in the address of his Excellency the President of the Republic at the opening of Congress; documents that have had a wider publication than the official journal can have. And yet attention is fixed on the silence of this journal, not taking into account the decided disapproval recorded in documents of the highest official character and the most notorious publicity. When such charges are sustained, nothing less than an ultimatum could give them weight.

What has now been said will enable Mr. Pareja to perceive that the Government of Chile, perfectly convinced of the rectitude of its proceedings and of the fairness of its policy with respect to the Government of H. C. M., cannot confess itself culpable of imaginary wrongs to Spain, nor accept the indecorous and humiliating proposal made to it of saluting the Spanish flag; a proposal which it rejects peremptorily and with lively disgust.

The intimations contained in Mr. Pareja's note leave it to be understood that the present reply will determine the Commander-in-Chief of the Spanish squadron to put in exercise measures of hostility against the Republic. Consequently the undersigned, in the name of his Government, protests at once earnestly and solemnly against such measures, that will be contrary to the spirit of the treaty existing between Chile and Spain, that will be the signal for open war between the two countries, and that will involve a scandalous abuse of power, all the tremendous responsibilty of which belongs to the aggressor.

If such an emergency shall arrive, the Republic, sustained by the justice of its own cause, supported by the heroism of its sons, taking God for judge, and the civilized world for a witness of the contest, will defend its honor and rights to the last extremity, and will carry on the war in all the methods which the law of nations permits, however extreme and painful they may be.

The undersigned offers to this end to Mr. Pareja, the tokens of his distinguished consideration.

ALVARO COVARRUBIAS.

To THE COMMANDER-IN-CHIEF *of the Spanish Squadron in the Pacific, and Plenipotentiary ad hoc of H. C. M.*

5

No. 4.

Admiral Pareja's Final Note to the Chilian Government.

FLAG SHIP, PACIFIC SQUADRON.

The undersigned, Commander-in-Chief of the Squadron of H. C. M. in the Pacific, and Minister Plenipotentiary to treat with the Government of Chile, has had this day the honor to receive, at 5 P. M., the note which Mr. Covarrubias, Secretary of State for Foreign Affairs, has directed to him in reply to his despatch of the 17th instant, and informed by its perusal that the Government of Santiago refuses the just satisfaction therein asked for offences given by Chile to Spain, is bound to state to him, in obedience to instructions of his Government, that if at 6 A. M. of the 24th, the Government of the Republic has not acceded to said request, the diplomatic relations between Chile and Spain will be ruptured, and the undersigned will find himself in the painful necessity of appealing, after that term has expired, to the force which he has under his command, to procure the satisfaction which the Government of Santiago declines giving, as the undersigned would have desired, by pacific measures.

The undersigned renews to Mr. Covarrubias the declaration which he framed at the close of his former note, viz., that he shall consider himself in duty bound, use of the force under his command having been made, to exact indemnification both for any losses sustained by his forces and for all the damage that may accrue to the persons, or property, or goods of subjects of H. C. M. residing in Chile; although, as he intimated in the line following, he hopes, whatever may be the course of events, that the Government of Chile will know how to prevent every kind of attempts unbecoming civilized nations.

The undersigned renews to Mr. Covarrubias the testimony of his distinguished consideration.

On board of the *Villa de Madrid*, in the port of Valparaiso, half-past seven, P. M., September 22, 1865.

JOSE MANUEL PAREJA.

To THE MINISTER OF FOREIGN AFFAIRS OF CHILE.

No. 5.

Final Note of the Chilian Government.

DEPARTMENT OF FOREIGN AFFAIRS OF CHILE,

SANTIAGO, *September* 23, 1865.

The undersigned, Secretary of State for Foreign Affairs, acknowledges receipt of the note of Mr. Pareja, Commander-in-Chief, etc., etc., dated yesterday at half past seven P. M., which came this day to hand, at eight A. M. In this communication Mr. Pareja insists on his demand for satisfaction, already rejected by the Government of Chile, and announces that if on the ·24th instant, at six A. M., assent has not been given thereto, he will resort to the force which he has under his command in order to obtain his claims. At the same time he declares anew that, once force having been employed, he shall exact indemnification for the losses that may result to the squadron, as well as for all damages that Spanish residents may sustain in their persons or interests in the Republic.

The undersigned hastens to fulfill the instructions of his Government, reiterating to Mr. Pareja the unalterable resolution of the Republic not to submit to the dishonorable and unjustifiable terms which have been proposed to it. Chile never will purchase peace at the cost of her dignity and her rights.

Mr. Pareja stands, therefore, in readiness to consummate to-morrow the acts of force which he may have in view, and to give the sad spectacle of an assault between nations which the conscience of civilized countries will know how to qualify and censure severely, and whose bitter fruits his own country will not be long in gathering.

However, Mr. Pareja greatly deceives himself if he founds any serious expectation on his afore-mentioned scheme of indemnification. The Government of the Republic, from the outset, rejects, whatever may be the contingencies of the future, every demand for compensation originated by the employment of force that the chief of the Spanish squadron may make. Furthermore, although Mr. Pareja has no right to invoke the practice of civilized nations, while preparing to exercise the act of violence which justice and civilization combine to condemn, the Government of the Republic will know how to fulfill the duties which honor, public faith, and international law imposes upon it.

The entire and exclusive responsibility of the incalculable evils which the conflict at hand will bring to the Government of Chile, and to the inhabitants of the country, natives as well as foreigners, must rest on the aggressor, on the Government of Spain and her agents, who are attempting to submit the Republic to proceedings the most vexatious with no just reason, with no decorous and plausible pretext, violating international law and right, and trampling on the most honored and respected usages of polished nations. Consequently, the Government of the undersigned will claim the fullest and most complete satisfaction for all damages and injuries by the most efficient means, and with that energy that belongs to the right.

While thus making this intimation in the most decided manner possible to Mr. Pareja, the undersigned again protests, and protests a thousand and one times, against every act of hostility whatever, which your squadron may direct against the Republic, and which will immediately produce open war between Chile and Spain.

The undersigned reiterates to Mr. Pareja the assurances of his distinguished consideration.

ALVARO COVARRUBIAS.

To the Commander, &c. &c., and Plenipotentiary *ad hoc of H. C. M.*

CORRESPONDENCE BETWEEN THE DIPLOMATIC CORPS AND ADMIRAL PAREJA.

No. 6.

First note of the Diplomatic Corps to Admiral Pareja

The Government of the Republic of Chile having communicated to the undersigned, members of the Diplomatic Corps, resident in Santiago, the following documents:

1st. The note dated the 17th instant, addressed by Admiral Pareja, Plenipotentiary of Her Catholic Majesty, to the Minister of Foreign Relations of the Republic of Chile.

2d. The power conferred by Her Majesty the Queen of Spain upon Admiral Pareja.

3d. The reply, dated the 21st instant, of the Minister of Foreign Relations of Chile to Admiral Pareja.

The undersigned have perceived in these documents, with regret, that a rupture between Chile and Spain is imminent, without any effort having been made for the amicable settlement of the pending difficulties, although the usages established among civilized nations require this latter mode of procedure, and although the power cited No. 2, peremptorily prescribe the opening of negotiations as the means of arriving at a reconciliation, as manifest from the following expressions:

" — may be necessary to enter into treaties with the said Republic," etc..... " that you may confer and agree upon, with the Plenipotentiary whom the President of Chile may name, that which may be most right and opportune......"

In the interest of Chile and Spain, and of their own respective countries, the undersigned hope that Admiral Pareja and the Government of the Republic, without regard to the terms of the notes exchanged, may yet open negotiations, in the serious intention of arriving at a pacific solution of the pending questions.

In the event that this legitimate hope should be frustrated, considering the damage to which the commerce of their respective nations, who had trusted for the preservation of peace in the arrangement of the 20th of May last, would be exposed by a sudden rupture between Chile and Spain, and awaiting instructions, the undersigned reserve to their Governments the adoption of such measures as they may deem necessary to take, in the interests of their respective nations.

At the same time the undersigned, in these exceptional circumstances, solemnly protest against any hostile act prejudicial to the persons or to the property of their respective nations.

The undersigned have signed this act in triplicate, whereof one copy will be transmitted to the Minister of Foreign Relations of the Republic, another to Admiral Pareja, and the third be deposited among the archives of their Dean, the Minister Plenipotentiary of the United States of America.

Done at Santiago, the 22d September, 1865.

(Signed)   THOMAS H. NELSON,
Envoy Extraordinary and Minister Plenipotentiary of the United States of America.

ANTONIO FERRO,
Minister Resident of the United States of Colombia.

HERMOJENES DE IRISARRI,
Charge d'Affairs of the Republic of Guatemala.

WILLIAM TAYLOUR THOMPSON,
Charge d'Affairs of Her Britannic Majesty.

LEVENHAGEN,
Charge d'Affairs of His Majesty the King of Prussia.

FLORY,
Consul General and Charge d'Affairs of France.

No. 7.

Translation of a telegraphic despatch, sent to Valparaiso, September 22, 1865, at 4.20 P. M., to Admiral Pareja.

To his Excellency JOSE MANUEL PAREJA, *Commander General of the Spanish Squadron in the Pacific, etc., etc., etc. :*

As the Dean of the Diplomatic Corps residing in Santiago, I have the honor to announce to your Excellency that the mail which will leave here this afternoon will convey to you a communication adopted by the said Corps and relating to the approaching interruption of the peace between Spain and Chile.

Permit me to beg that your Excellency postpone the adoption of any measure of hostility until you shall have received the communication referred to.

I have the honor to be your Excellency's obedient servant,

THOMAS H. NELSON,
Envoy Extraordinary and Minister Plenipotentiary of the United States of America.

No. 8.

Reply by telegraph from Valparaiso, September 22, 1865, 7 P. M.

HON. THOMAS H. NELSON :

I have had an interview with Admiral Pareja, and he has assured me that he will take no step whatever until he has received the communication mentioned in your telegraphic despatch.　　　　　　　AMBROSE W. CLARK.

No. 9.

Admiral Pareja's first reply to the Diplomatic Corps.

FLAGSHIP OF THE PACIFIC SQUADRON.

The undersigned, Commander-in Chief of the Squadron of H. C. M. in the Pacific and also Her Minister Plenipotentiary, has had the honor to receive the joint note of the Diplomatic Corps resident in Santiago, which the Representative of the United States of America, Dean of the said Corps in the Republic of Chile, has been pleased to transmit him through his consul in Valparaiso.

The public ministers who sign it express therein the same re gret that is experienced by the undersigned at the rupture due to the obstinacy of the Government of the Republic in not ac ceding by pacific means to the reparation it owes to that of H. C. M. for offences committed against her, which this latter cannot overlook consistently with her honor.

In replying to the said note, it is the duty of the undersigned to manifest to the Diplomatic Corps, through its Dean, that the notes exchanged between Messrs. Tavira and Covarrubias, as well those of last year as during May of the present, in relation to the said offences, prove that, on the part of Spain, the necessary efforts have been made to arrange amicably the conflict caused by the Government of Chile in offering those offences, and that the Government of H. C. M. not having accepted, as it could not accept, the explanation admitted in May by Mr. Tavira, no other course remained, towards that of the Republic, than to demand peremptorily that reparation, to which she is most clearly entitled. And it is evident that the undersigned, having been named to replace Mr. Tavira, the only course he could take was to present to the Government of Santiago the said demand in the terms named by him, adhering strictly therein to the instructions of his Government. Therefore, if by various notes an attempt has been made to arrange amicably the difficulties, and the Government of Spain has not considered the evasions presented by that of Chile in May last, as reparation, it had a right to demand peremptorily that reparation, and neither it nor its representative have in this case departed in the least from the diplomatic usages of civilized countries.

The undersigned will deplore as much as the public ministers to whom he has the honor to address himself, the inevitable losses which hostilities against Chile must cause to trade, but be it permitted to him to manifest to them the assurance which he feels, that if any one of their respective Governments had received from that of Chile the offences and injuries which the latter has inflicted upon that of Spain they would have acted in a similar manner; that is, they would by no means have deemed the evasions presented in its notes of May last as a reparation. Consequently the results which these notes would have might be easily presumed, especially since Mr. Tavira, in expressing himself satisfied with the explanations given therein, says in his own of the 20th of that month, " do away, *in my opinion*, with all the motives of complaint which my Government entertained," an evident proof that such conformity, on the part of Mr. Tavira, by no means bound his Government, and consequently it could not inspire confidence in the preservation of peace.

The undersigned regrets, therefore, being unable to gratify the hope of the Diplomatic Corps resident in Santiago without failing to appreciate at its full value the effort which, responding to their noble mission, they have made in their note to avoid a rupture between Chile and Spain.

The undersigned will not conclude without manifesting to the Foreign Public Ministers, resident in Santiago, in order that they may be able to appreciate at their full value the just causes which have moved the Government of Spain to place her question with Chile upon its present footing, that he transmits to them herein a copy of the *memorandum* which that Government has instructed him to forward to those of the other Spanish American Republics, in the event of a rupture with Chile, and as it is to be feared that the Government of this Republic, according to the tenor of the note received from it yesterday, will not accede to the demand for reparation, which he has repeated to it in the ultimatum forwarded last night, whose term expires to-morrow morning at six o'clock, that rupture, if the negative be again confirmed, will take place from that hour.

The undersigned avails himself of this opportunity to offer to

6

the Diplomatic Corps resident in Santiago and to its Honorable Dean, the assurance of his most elevated consideration and respect.

On Board of the *Villa de Madrid*, in the port Valparaiso. September 23d, 1865.

JOSE MANUEL PAREJA.

To His Excellency, the Envoy Extraordinary and Minister Plenipotentiary of the United States, near the Government of Chile, and the Dean of the Diplomatic Corps in Santiago.

No. 10.

Second Note from the Diplomatic Corps to Admiral Pareja.

The undersigned, members of the Diplomatic Corps, resident in Santiago, have seen with regret in the note of the 23d instant, which Mr. Pareja, Commander-in-Chief of the squadron of her Catholic Majesty in the Pacific and her Plenipotentiary, has been pleased to address them, that his Excellency persists in resting his demands upon armed force, without endeavoring beforehand to attain the aim of his mission by conciliatory measures.

The undersigned do not believe themselves called upon to emit an opinion in regard to the motives which determined the Government of H. C. M. to demand satisfaction from the Government of Chile; they desire only to prevent an unnecessary rupture between the two countries, which but a short time since were in relations of a friendly character, and to which their own are bound by numerous interests. For this reason the undersigned permitted themselves, a few days since, to express to his Excellency their hope that in accordance with the terms of the power conferred upon him, and guided by pacific desires, he would open negotiations with the Government of the Republic. They do not partake of his opinion that nothing remained for him but to make peremptory demands; the explanations given to Mr. Tavira by the Minister of Foreign Relations of Chile, in his note of the 16th of May last, satisfied the Representative of Her Catholic Majesty; from that moment an arrangement between the two countries was concluded; the differences which had for some time past cooled their relations ceased to exist, and Mr. Tavira, having acted in the capacity of Minister of Her Catholic Majesty, there was the right to believe that the arrangement accepted by him would be ratified by her Court. The disapproval which it met with replaces the two parties interested in the same position in which they were before the beginning of the first negotiations, and there was conse- quently room for their re opening.

In conformity with this rule of diplomacy as well as of com- mon law, the note of 17th instant, which the Commander-in- Chief has addressed to the Minister of Foreign Relations of the Republic, says :

" It is the duty of the undersigned to reproduce, now, the " complaints already presented."

It further states, " motives of complaint—sufficiently justified " in the several notes of Mr. Tavira; and he limits himself to " consider them as reproduced in this communication, comply- " ing therein with the orders of the Government of H. C. " Majesty." And further on :

" The Government of Her Catholic Majesty considers that " the state of affairs is the same that existed when Mr. Tavira " addressed his note of the 13th of May last to Mr. Covarrubias."

The Commander-in-Chief, in his note of the 17th, refers to that of Mr. Tavira of 13th May last, taking it as a point of departure for negotiation ; but, instead of awaiting the reply which the Minister of Chile might have given him under the present circumstances, His Excellency adds to the demands made by Mr. Tavira and threatens the Government of the Republic with hostilities, if within the term of a few days it should not grant what he demands. His Excellency presents an ultimatum before opening negotiations.

The undersigned have reason to believe that the Government of the Republic would not have refused to give satisfactory explanations, if the Commander-in-Chief had made any effort to arrange amicably the existing difficulties ; but it was impossible that it should accede to the demands made at once in a threatening tone by a peremptory ultimatum.

The undersigned, resting upon the reasons set forth above, reiterate the expression of their hope that negotiations will be again opened looking to a pacific solution of the existing difficulties. Should acts of hostility take place before the means of conciliation have been exhausted, the undersigned will find themselves obliged to maintain the reservations and the protestations which they have already presented in their note of the 22d instant.

The undersigned avail themselves of this occasion to offer to His Excellency the Commander-in-Chief and Minister Plenipotentiary of H. C. M. the assurance of their high consideration.

(Signed)   THOMAS H. NELSON,
Envoy Extraordinary and Minister Plenipotentiary of the United States of America.

ANTONIO FERRO,
Minister Resident of the United States of Colombia.

HERMOJENES DE IRISARRI,
Charge d'Affairs of the Republic of Guatemala.

WILLIAM TAYLOUR THOMPSON,
Charge d'Affairs of Her Britannic Majesty.

LEVENHAGEN,
Charge d'Affairs of His Majesty the King of Prussia.

FLORY,
Consul General and Charge d'Affairs of France.

P. S.—At the moment when the undersigned were about to address this note to His Excellency, they learn that he had already declared hostilities. It only remains for them therefore to refer to the final paragraph of the same.

No. 11.

Translation of a Telegraph Despatch sent to Valparaiso on the 23d September, at 12½ o'clock.

SANTIAGO, *September* 24.

JOSE MANUEL PAREJA, *Commander-in-Chief of the Spanish Squadron in the Pacific, etc. etc.*

[Care of the United States Consul.]

As Dean of the Diplomatic Corps, I have the honor to acknowledge the receipt of your Excellency's note of this date, at the same time announcing one from said Corps, which your Excellency will receive to-morrow.

I dare to hope that your Excellency will suspend the employment of hostilities against the Republic of Chile until the receipt of the communication announced.

I have the honor to be, your Excellency's obedient serv't,

THOMAS H. NELSON.

No. 12.

Reply to the foregoing, received in Santiago, at 9 A. M., September 24, 1865.

VALPARAISO, *September* 24, 1865.

Hon. T. H. NELSON:

I received your dispatch and delivered it as soon as it was possible.

The reply is as follows:

FLAG SHIP OF THE SQUADRON.

Honorable Mr. NELSON, *Dean of the Diplomatic Corps in Santiago:*

The Commander-in-Chief of the squadron of H. C. Majesty manifests to Mr. Nelson, that the Government of Chile having replied last night to the ultimatum which he had addressed to it, hostilities have already begun. He has the honor to be your Excellency's obedient servant.

JOSE M. PAREJA.

" *Villa de Madrid,*" September 24, 1865.

A. W. CLARK.

No. 13.

Note from the Chilian Minister of Foreign Affairs to the Minister of the United States.

DEPARTMENT OF FOREIGN RELATIONS, REPUBLIC OF CHILE,
SANTIAGO, *September* 23, 1865.

The undersigned, Minister of Foreign Relations of Chile, has had the honor to receive the note dated yesterday, which the Envoy Extraordinary and Minister Plenipotentiary of the United States of North America has been pleased to address to him, transmitting him the despatch of the meeting held yesterday by the Diplomatic Corps, resident in this Capital.

In the name of his Government, the undersigned offers his sincere thanks to the Minister Plenipotentiary and to his Honorable Colleagues, for the interest with which they have viewed the complication which in these moments threatens to bring about a rupture between Chile and Spain.

The Diplomatic Corps has observed and deplored with much reason, that this rupture should not have been preceded by any effort whatever, on the part of the Chief of the Spanish Squadron, to amicably discuss the differences. Such an omission is so much the more strange, and to be regretted, inasmuch as the Government of Chile has never refused to explain its acts, convinced as it is of never having offered any offence to either the honor or legitimate interests of Spain.

Nevertheless, in order to revive an extinct question, it has been preferred to abandon all the paths to conciliation ; the first step has been to present a peremptory ultimatum and exact in a threatening tone, satisfactory explanations, which the Government of Chile has never refused, and a salute of amends which is founded upon no effective grievance, and the Republic has been thus fatally placed between a rupture or an unmerited humiliation. The choice cannot be doubtful for a Government which knows how to respect the dignity of its country and its own.

The new communication which the undersigned has to-day received from Mr. Pareja, renders so painful an extremity still more imminent, since it re aggravates the former ultimatum and announces the proximate employment of measures of hostility.

The responsibility of the mournful consequences which these

47

measures must bring with them, belongs only to the Chief of the
Spanish Squadron, and to the Government of Her Catholic
Majesty, which has authorized an aggression, unjustifiable in its
antecedents, its form, and its object.

The undersigned avails himself of this occasion to reiterate to
the Envoy Extraordinary and Minister Plenipotentiary of the
United States of North America, the expression of his sentiments
of distinguished consideration and regard.

ALVARO COVARRUBIAS.

*To the Envoy Extraordinary and Minister Plenipotentiary of
the U. S. of North America.*

No. 14.

PETITION OF THE MERCHANTS OF VALPARAISO TO THE DIPLOMATIC CORPS.

Signed by 53 of the largest Foreign Commercial Houses of Valparaiso.

VALPARAISO, *September* 27, 1865.

To the Honorable Members of the
Foreign Diplomatic Body, *Santiago:*

GENTLEMEN,—We, the undersigned members of the Foreign
Commercial Body of Valparaiso, take the liberty of address-
ing you collectively regarding the serious position in which we
have been placed through the proceedings of Admiral Pareja,
Commanding the Spanish Squadron on this coast.

We need not occupy your attention with a recital of the
serious losses we have already incurred from these proceedings.
We would simply say that the consequences of Admiral Pareja's
measures, if persisted in, will bring utter ruin upon many of our
number and those whom we represent.

We beg in the strongest manner to express our conviction
that measures of so highhanded injustice, undertaken without
adequate warning, are contrary to the rights and duties of the

representatives of civilized nations; a conviction which we understand is shared in by yourselves, and one which we trust will be made effectual ground for the exaction of substantial reparation.

We are not aware what Admiral Pareja's intentions are with respect to foreign property in this port or afloat in this bay, after the expiration of the ten days' notice, and we entertain serious fears that, under the plea of inflicting injury on Chile, our interests are those which are to be sacrificed.

Impressed by these and other considerations, the Foreign Commercial Body, at a meeting held this day, unanimously resolved to address you collectively to suggest that all the foreign force under your influence or command in these seas be brought to this port without delay for the protection of our interests. They, moreover, resolved to be at the cost of placing one of the steamers of the English Line at your disposal, should it be deemed necessary by you, for the more speedy and effectual carrying out of your views for our protection, whatever these may be.

We have the honor to remain, gentlemen,
Your most obedient humble servants,

WILLIAM GIBBS & Co.
WEBER & Co.
WILLIAMSON, BALFOUR & Co.
VORWERK & Co.
MACK & Co.
POISSON & Co.
J. H. PEARSON.
FEHRMAN, FISCHER & Co.
F. HUTH GRUNING & Co.
ZAHN & Co.
MEEKS & BROWN.
E. MOMUS.
STOCKMEYER & SCHULTZ.
GEORGE GARLAND.
LE QUELLEC & BORDES.
LORING & Co.
E. DARNAY & Co.

HELSBY & Co.
ALSOP & Co.
MYERS, BLAND & Co.
GUNSTON, LEDWARD & Co.
HEATLEY & Co.
GRAHAM, ROWE & Co.
GREEN, NICHOLSON & Co.
HENDERSON & Co.
JOHN THOMPSON WATSON & Co.
THOS. BLAND GARLAND.
FERREIRA & AGGAR.
N. C. SCHUTH.
CHOPIS.
WILMS & SOTHERS.
R. J. CLAUSSEN.
T. LACHAMBRE & Co.
ROSE, INNES & Co.

Morris Thompson & Co.
Antony & Meric.
A. Hemenway & Co.
Sawers, Duncan & Co.
Templeman & Co.
Panulcillo Copper Co.
Queille B. & Co.
Julio Merlet.
Betteley & Co.
Mongiardini & Co.

Hainsworth & Co.
D. Schutte Droste & Co.
Robert Walker.
Luis Osthaus.
Cooper & Co.
D. Sim.
Germain Brothers.
Miller, Cox & Co.
P. Soruco & Co.

The following additional Correspondence has been received since the foregoing was in type.

United States Legation,
Santiago, Oct. 7, 1865.

Sir,—Having learned with much pleasure of your arrival at Valparaiso in order to resume your functions as Minister Resident of his Majesty the Emperor of Brazil to the government of Chili, I have the honor to transmit for your information a copy of the correspondence that has passed between the diplomatic corps resident at Santiago, and the Commandant-in-Chief of her Catholic Majesty's squadron in the Pacific.

Your obedient servant,
Thomas H. Nelson.

To his Excellency Francisco A. De Varnhagen, Minister Resident, &c.

Legation of the Empire of Brazil,
Santiago, Oct. 9, 1865.

Sir,—I have the honor to acknowledge the receipt of your Excellency's communication, transmitting on behalf of the diplomatic corps accredited to this republic, copies of the three joint notes dated on 22d, 24th, and 28th of September last, and addressed in my absence by the said diplomatic corps to the commandant of her Catholic Majesty's squadron at Valparaiso.

I beg to thank you for your courteous communication, and in reply I must state that, had I been here at the time, I should have had great pleasure in joining my signature to those of my worthy colleagues upon the three notes mentioned. I take advantage of this occasion to add that, after deciding to leave Peru and accept the mission to this republic, although I feared, from

7

certain information communicated to me at Lima and Callao, that the questions pending between Chili and Spain might become complicated, I never thought it possible that an open rupture could occur in so short a time. On the contrary, I did not conceive that a rupture could take place before the commandant of her Catholic Majesty's squadron had presented the autograph letter of his sovereign accrediting him as her plenipotentiary, and without a fresh investigation of old grievances, inasmuch as a royal decree had lately been issued, commenting in no favorable terms upon the action of the minister who had revised these differences and presented unjustifiable claims.

Although I come at a late moment to associate myself with my colleagues in their noble efforts in behalf of peace, and in defence of the rights of civilization, I hope that our good offices, and those of our respective governments, whether collectively or separately, may prove effective as soon as the government of her Catholic Majesty shall receive more accurate information from impartial judges concerning all that has occured, showing that this war (which is now causing more detriment to foreign commerce and subjects than to the Chilians themselves, who are, as I see, determined to uphold their honor and their rights at all hazards) must cause great loss and damage to Spanish shipping, not only in the waters of the Pacific, but on the coasts of Europe and the Antilles.

I shall communicate all the foregoing in detail to my government, which is well informed of my sentiments towards Spain, as I resided there eleven years, passing seven of them at Madrid as the representative of my country, and during that time I gave ample proofs of my conciliatory and amicable feelings, as well as of a sacred respect for truth and justice.

I have the v   honor to be your Excellency's most obedient servant,

A. De Varnhagen.

To his Excellency Senor Thomas H. Nelson, Envoy Extraordinary and Minister Plenipotentiary of the United States of America, and Representative of the Diplomatic Corps resident at Santiago.

www.ingramcontent.com/pod-product-compliance
Lightning Source LLC
Chambersburg PA
CBHW031813090426
42739CB00008B/1257